How To Start A Record Label

A Step By Step Guide

By

**Darrell Ballard
(AKA DINK)**

authorHOUSE

1663 LIBERTY DRIVE, SUITE 200
BLOOMINGTON, INDIANA 47403
(800) 839-8640
www.authorhouse.com

© 2004 Darrell Ballard.
All Rights Reserved.

No part of this book may be reproduced, stored in a retrieval system, or transmitted by any means without the written permission of the author.

First published by AuthorHouse 07/02/04

ISBN: 1-4184-5899-6 (e)
ISBN: 1-4184-4906-7 (sc)

Printed in the United States of America
Bloomington, Indiana

This book is printed on acid-free paper.

DEDICATION

This book is dedicated to you DaShya for your unconditional love and patience while I've been away. You've always stood by me when others were in doubt, this one's for you.

Love Dad

"THE ULTIMATE LUXURY IN LIFE IS CHOICE"

ACKNOWLEDGEMENTS

I would like to thank all the people, groups and artists who were involved in my struggles, growths, experiences and successes.

Special thanks to you Too Short for the opportunity of doing my first video and for taking a chance on me as a new comer and introducing me to so many people.

Special thanks to Lil Jon and the East Side Boyz for giving me my personal tour of Atlanta. Thank you for introducing me to the Young Bloods of the Attic crew, Ludacris, Jim Crow, Emperor Searcy of hot 97 & Greg Street of V103 and Luke of 2 Live Crew.

Also a special thanks to Nelly and the St Lunatics for believing in me for their very first video.

Thank you Chad for introducing me to the twins, Chris & Conrad of Bread & Water.

Thank you Donni Redd of "Who You Callin Country"

Thank you Blast and Scarecrow of Frontline.

Thank you to DJ's Kool Kaos & Tossing Ted of 100.3 the beat radio station in St. Louis.

Thank you to 40 Grand and Jacque Land, President of 100 Black men in St. Louis.

Thank you to BET and VH1 for showing my work.

Thank you to Carmen Lovelace my secretary.

Thank you Baby D and Quentin Black of Short Records.

Thank you to my mom's friend Velma Ivy, who was gracious enough to edit my book.

And last but not least, Yusef Muhammed, for the great work you did on the videos I couldn't have done it without you.

Also to the brothers Eugene (Geno) Martin and Garland Cantrell Spivey, thanks for staying in my corner.

A very very special thanks to the women in my life who stuck by me through it all, my mom Diane Ballard, the one person who believed in me no matter what with her unconditional love and support. My daughter DaShya Ballard, I'm so very glad you were born to me, my love for you is what keeps me sane.

Thanks to all my clients past and present and to those of you who kept asking "When are you going to finish the book ?" Here it is, enjoy!

Table Of Contents

DEDICATION v
"THE ULTIMATE LUXURY IN LIFE IS CHOICE" vi
ACKNOWLEDGEMENTS vii
FOREWARD x
A WORD FROM THE AUTHOR xi
CHAPTER 1 REGISTERING YOUR BUSINESS 1
CHAPTER 2 PRODUCING PRODUCT 7
CHAPTER 3 COPYRIGHT AND PUBLISHING 12
CO-PUBLISHING AGREEMENTS 15
CHAPTER 4 VINYL 12" INCH ALBUM 19
CHAPTER 5 CD DESIGN, POSTERS, FLATS, T-SHIRTS, ETC. 23
CHAPTER 6 COMPLETING YOUR CD MANUFACTURING AND PRESSING 27
CHAPTER 7 ADVERTISING 31
CHAPTER 8 CD RELEASE DATE 36
CHAPTER 9 CD RELEASE PARTY 40
CHAPTER 10 SOME OF THE MOST FREQUENTLY ASKED QUESTIONS. 44
OTHER BOOKS BY THE AUTHOR INCLUDE 52

FOREWARD

My inspiration for this book is to inform all of you who are interested in starting your own record label.

I've worked with many artists, groups, record labels and radio stations. I've done concert promotions, music videos, written songs, movies and books. I also had a record label called "Street Life Records". I have gained much knowledge and experience about the industry by working closely with all of these special entertainers. Through this experience I became a Music Consultant, spoke at Music Seminars, and gave advice on numerous occasions to people all over the U.S. Everyone should be so fortunate to love and enjoy your work as I do.

This book is for all of you who want to learn about the industry.

Let's get started!

A WORD FROM THE AUTHOR

This book was written with the purpose of educating individuals on "How to Start a Record Label". The knowledge of what an individual will need to start their own label is in this book. During my days of trying to start my own label I searched for such a book, a blue print of sorts to tell me what steps to take and in what order, I couldn't find any. After years of success with my own company, I decided to give back.

People from all over the U.S. have come to me for advice on how to start a record label of their own. After a while I found I kept repeating myself so I decided to put together a guide that could help those in search of the knowledge to get started on their own label. You will also find the name of a music consulting company that I have listed to help you if you get off track.

If you are ready for the knowledge to own your record label then proceed forward!

CHAPTER 1
REGISTERING YOUR BUSINESS

"Life is a never-ending journey in which learning is also never ending. In order to continue to live you must continue to learn. Once you've stopped learning you've stopped living. One needs a variety of understanding to live in this life time."

From the book "Words of Wisdom"
by
Darrell (Dink) Ballard

The first step is to register your business name. Like other existing businesses, e.g., barbershops, car washes, etc., you want to register as a Corporation not a regular business because you'll reap more benefits, I won't go into details at this moment because that would change the lesson here. For more details about that order the book, "<u>Benefits of Incorporating.</u>" Those benefits are for tax purposes and more.

Your next step is to contact your City Hall to ensure that you go directly to the right place saving you time and money because time is money. Once you contact them find out if you're in the right place to get a license for your company to incorporate your business! Inquire about the cost to register as a corporation. The cost should be approximately $50-$150 (each city varies).

Once you have registered your corporation you will be asked to fill out a form called Articles of Incorporation, asking you about your particular business. What type of business are you incorporating?

Who are the owners of your corporation? Where will you and the business be registered as far as address, city, and state is concerned, and name of your business?

Once you've completed the forms, they will run a name check to ensure no other company has the same name. No two corporations are allowed the same name, but two regular businesses can, that's one of the benefits of incorporating.

Once all the checks are done and the paperwork has been correctly filled out and paid for they will give you what is called an "entity identification number" known as an EIN or Federal Tax ID number.

Darrell Ballard

After you receive your EIN number take it to the bank of your choice and open your corporate bank account. An EIN is like a social security number, it is the social security of corporations. Once you get established, you will be getting all of your corporation necessities under your corporate name.

Let's say you want to open an account with another company or get a loan, you will be asked your E.I.N. number so that the credit of your corporation will be checked, not your credit under your personal social security number.

Your corporation is like a separate person with its own social security number. After you open your corporate account call and get your corporate telephone line opened under your corporate E.I.N. After you've got your corporate account and telephone number, go to the post office and get a P. O. box under your corporate name.

The benefit of having a corporate telephone is no matter where you move within the city you can keep the same number. The purpose of having the P.O. box is to continue to get your mail anywhere you move. The best place to get a P. O. box is downtown in your local city or the post office in your local area.

"The person who knows can take risks, the person who doesn't know can't take risks."

Darrell Ballard

"Be prepared: the person armed with wisdom will not be attacked by foolishness. The shortest way out is to divide your life out wisely, life is painful without rest. What makes life pleasant is a variety of learning. Live neither entirely for others nor entirely for yourself. If you are wise you will understand people seek you not for your sake but for their own."

CHAPTER 2
PRODUCING PRODUCT

Darrell Ballard

"Many people behave not according to who they are but how people expect them to be."

How To Start A Record Label

Now that you have registered your corporation the next step is product. The music you make is your product.

Maybe some of you already have your product, maybe not. One question that I'm frequently asked is how many songs should be on the first album? I suggest 12 but that's really up to the owner. Now what you must remember is most people are trying to eventually get their music played on the radio. I suggest that you first concentrate on 3 songs. From the 3 songs you must decide which one is going to be your first single. Keep in mind that you will eventually go for getting this song on the radio. Ensure that one is a radio commercial version of the song. The reason I say make 3 songs first, because it's easier to choose your first single from 3 songs than it is from 12 songs.

Since you are the owner of this company it's obvious you get the last say about everything. I strongly suggest that you make yourself a copy of these 3 songs. You should have a copy of these 3 songs burned on CD, take them and get other people's opinions on the songs they think are the hottest and which one they think should be released first.

The reason for this is the public are the people that will be buying your music. Sometimes it's not about which song is the best, it's about which song will sell. I'm sure you're in this business to make money so keep this in mind. Once you've done your survey on which song to put out first, finish recording the album with the rest of the songs. The next phase will be to get vinyl made which will be discussed in the next chapter. Ensure that the name of the album and the name of those 3 songs are complete. This is very important because it will be needed for the next phase of your project.

"Don't grow too familiar with people or permit them to grow familiar with you, things are least respected when used the most."

"Keep something in reserve in all matters. You'll preserve your usefulness. Don't use all your talents at once or show all of your strengths all the time."

CHAPTER 3

COPYRIGHT AND PUBLISHING

Let's start off with a little information. Under the present Copyright Laws any original work that's in written format or recorded tape is automatically protected under the laws of copyright. Contact the Copyright office at (202) 707-9100 if you know what forms you need, if you don't know call (202) 707-3000. You can also send a written request to:

REGISTER OF COPYRIGHTS, LIBRARY OF CONGRESS, WASHINGTON D.C., 20559

Copyright forms that most song writers use for registering music and lyrics of a song is form PA, which stands for Performing Arts. A C indicates music and lyrics that are copyrighted. The label owner will need to register a recording of the song by using form SR which protects the "sound recording". This protects you from people copying the recording and using it. When a sound recording is copyrighted it is indicated by the symbol "P" next to the lyrics and music and provides protection for the owner.

Copyright applications are sent to the Library of Congress with the forms completed along with a $30.00 check or money order (which is the cost at the present) for each form sent and a copy of your song (s).

Registration is effective the day the copyright office receives your material (for best results send it certified mail).

Compulsory Mechanical Licenses are issued to those persons wanting to record and release copyright work. In order to get a C.M.L. the person or label wanting to do this must notify the copyright owner of their intentions to release the work before it's available for sale.

Darrell Ballard

"Be self-reliant, the person who knows himself overcomes his weakness with thoughtfulness and the wise manage to conquer all, even the stars."

CO-PUBLISHING AGREEMENTS

Song writing royalties comes from three sources and the diagram below should help you understand.

WRITER	WRITER
	LABEL

The song writer who creates the music and the publisher who markets the music splits the royalties 50/50. The publisher's share is 50% of the total copyright revenues, the other 50% goes to the writer. A publishers responsibility is issuing licenses for the use of songs and finding producers and artists to record and perform the song and also to ensure the royalties are paid. Don't forget, publishers usually get 50% of the total royalties.

The majority of independent labels get 50% of the publishers share. This is common with artists who write their own songs and this is called a co-publishing deal. The diagram shows the publisher's royalties are split 50/50 with the publisher and label. The songwriter gets 50% of the total royalties and 50% of the publishing share, which gives the songwriter a total of 75%. The label gets 25% of overall royalties.

Songwriter royalties - the record label pays mechanical royalties for the right to manufacture and sell the writer songs. Rates are approximately 8 cents per song per record sold.

Darrell Ballard

Performance royalties – are collected by the American Society of Composers, Authors and Publishers, known as (ASCAP). The Broadcast Music Incorporated is known as (BMI) or SESAC. These are the three organizations who issue licenses for the use of music written or published by their members. When the music is played or performed in public venues, like clubs, radio and television, they charge fees appropriate to the venue and distribute the royalties to the writers and publishers.

Synchronization royalties – are paid for the use of a song on TV shows, commercials, movies, etc.. This license has no set amount. A 50/50 co-publishing agreement between you as label owner and the artist and song writers give you 25% total.

Opening your publishing company – to collect publisher's royalties you must open a publishing company.

Songwriters must also open a publishing company to collect their royalties. You must have a publishing company to get the money for publishing royalties. To open a publishing company, you must submit a company name to

ASCAP, BMI or SECAP. Pick the company writers with all three and submit names of your company to each one separately. Ensure the name you submit isn't already being used. ASCAP charges about $50.00 a year, BMI charges a one-time fee of about $100.00 and SECAP doesn't charge a fee. Your publishing company must have an address and an account already set up. Incorporate it or get a Business Certificate. This is where your royalty checks will be deposited

For more information on the Recording Industry Association of America (RIAA) call (800) 223-2328 or (202) 775-0101.

"Don't waste favors on people who owe you. Keep important friends for a great time."

."Recognize the man of words from the man of deeds. It is a clever distinction, like the distinction between the friend who values your friendship for you and the one who values you for your position."

CHAPTER 4

VINYL 12" INCH ALBUM

One of the most important steps in music is vinyl. Most artists and groups miss this because it's rarely talked about, that's why it is overlooked. Vinyl is the album that your DJ's play at the clubs. You must find a vinyl company to print your single, a club version of the song with words that will not be allowed on the radio, and a radio version of the song. The significance of the vinyl is to make "Side A" the club version, the instrumental version and acappella version, on "Side B" the radio version. The purpose of the vinyl is to get your music playing in the most important places, the clubs, which are known as the Underground. I'd rather my music be playing in all the clubs than playing on all radio stations, but if you get it playing in the clubs all the radio stations will want to play it as well.

Now let's talk about that for a while. Most cities have a mix time on the radio. Who are the people on the mix hour? A DJ makes it is possible for you to hear a person's vocals on somebody else's music (instrumental) and somebody's instrumental playing with other people's vocals. So you become familiar with people's vocals and instrumentals.

Sometimes most mix DJ's on the radio are the same DJ's at the clubs. Whose music do the DJ's play on their mix time? The hottest artists, but basically whomever they want. See, a DJ at the radio station cannot play whatever they want, they can only play what is on the program selection! The program director picks his or her selection from the billboard chart, which shows the top 100 selling CD's, hottest artists and groups. We won't go into detail in that area at this moment. Stations cannot play whatever they want, they can only play what is on the program selection!

"Freedom starts in the mind. One is not truly free until ones mind is free. Knowledge is what frees the mind."

"The most important business is your own business."

CHAPTER 5

CD DESIGN, POSTERS, FLATS, T-SHIRTS, ETC.

Darrell Ballard

"Neither hate nor love forever. Treat your friends as though they are your enemies. It usually happens that way anyway."

Designing is a very important part of your advertising and promotions, if you don't advertise and promote your product then how do you expect people to know who you are to buy your music!

You must come up with the logo design for your CD cover so you can put it on your hats, T-shirts, etc. I suggest that whatever logo design you choose to put on your CD put that same design on your posters and flats (flats are similar to poster cards). Come up with something creative but remember that something simple and plain is also creative, so don't overdo your design. Remember prices vary because of design, amount ordered, and company to company. I suggest that what you do first is a "Coming Soon". You do the "coming soon" on your flats and your posters. The reason that *I* suggest this is because you still have a couple of weeks before the completion of the CD.

I recommend that you only get a minimum amount of T-shirts, posters and flats because you are only trying to create a buzz without spending a lot of money (approximately 100 T-shirts or less, 100-500 posters, 100-500 flats).

The flats and posters will cost $200- $500. You want to put these in places where a lot of people hang out, clubs, car wash, barbershops, beauty shops, etc. Remember the people who wear your T-shirts are actually promoting your music, so give them out strategically. Now let's go to the next phase which will be completing your CD.

"Every choice we make whether good or bad has consequences."

CHAPTER 6

COMPLETING YOUR CD MANUFACTURING AND PRESSING

We are back to the CD. Now how you finish the CD is very important. My suggestion is that you don't choose one producer for all the music on your CD or all the songs will sound too similar. You have to do a break down of your songs and divide them accordingly. Let's say you make songs for this group of people and more songs for another group of people, diversify your CD so you can cater specific songs to specific audiences, this makes your CD marketable to a larger crowd of people. You also have to find the right company to press up your CD with all the things that you want, specifically your UPC bar code.

Bar codes are used so that sound scan can calculate how many sales you are getting from the stores. This is really important to remember because a lot of pressing companies don't offer UPC bar codes, that is why some companies press CD's so much cheaper than others, cheaper is not always better. I'd rather make sure that my product is produced correctly the first time. It will end up costing you more in the long run to correct the problems. Most companies will return your CD's in 4 to 6 weeks. It's best that you do all of your design work because you will save yourself money. On the first CD I would recommend a two (2) sleeve insert which is the front and back of the CD.

This is more cost effective. Now for those who have the extra money, go ahead if you like and use the 4 page inserts. But remember you are in this business to make money. So the more you save the more you make. There are plenty of manufacturing and pressing companies out there. Make sure you choose one that meets all of your requirements.

"You cannot change the past but your future is spotless."

"A short cut to becoming a true person is to put the right people beside you. Intelligence is transferred much easier."

CHAPTER 7

ADVERTISING

"Common sense is not always common."

Advertising is one of the most important parts of any business or company. If you don't advertise then how will you get your product out to the public?

The most frequently asked question "what's the best way to advertise?" My suggestion is one you can afford i.e., radio, television, magazines, internet, and word-of-mouth advertisement. The benefit of being a consultant to many companies, artists and groups is you have plenty of connections. Now I really like television advertising.

Television is the most powerful form of advertising because it lets you see the face behind the voice. Most people are recognized by their voice and not by face. One of the companies I consult (Commercials Express) was formed for that reason to help independent companies, labels and groups to get recognized. The address is located in the back of this book. Remember you have already started with your posters, flats and T-shirts. Now you can use your commercials for the "Coming Soon" CD or your "In Stores Now" CD. Because I consult for Commercials

Express, all you have to do is mention that you got their address and phone number from this book and they will give you a discount on all of your commercials. I highly recommend Commercial Express.

Imagine seeing a commercial for your label, group or song on B.E.T., MTV, USA, TNT or TBS.

These are some of the stations that Commercials Express can put your commercial on, we can get in more detail by calling or writing. Now let's move to the next phase which will be your CD release date.

"Success is the best revenge."

"If you don't have a backup plan you don't have a plan at all."

CHAPTER 8
CD RELEASE DATE

"Know yourself, your intellect, character, emotion and judgment. You can't master yourself if you don't understand yourself."

Darrell Ballard

Your CD release date is very important, it's the date you officially have for your CD's to be sold in stores. Even though you may have CD's already in stores and they've been selling, it is important to sell as many as you possibly can on the CD release date out of stores. Your CD's will be calculated onto sound scan which will be related to billboard. The first impression is very important. If you can sell all 1000 CD's on this date the better and whatever is left over from the original 1000 ordered. The more you sell, the more your music is being heard and circulated, the more people will want your music. This is also the day that all of your advertising has led up to and is the most important advertising day that you have.

"Be careful about information. Your ears are the back door of truth and the front door of deceit. Truth is better seen than heard."

CHAPTER 9
CD RELEASE PARTY

"Freedom never came free."

Darrell Ballard

Now it's time to have some fun. A party is to celebrate the release of the CD. By now your CD's are back from the manufacturing and pressing company. Do not throw a CD release party until you have your CD's in your possession. For this you will need a venue, a place to have your release party, which could be at a club, lounge, hall, etc. You want to set it up like a small concert to give people a chance to see your group perform a small amount of their album. I would suggest a (10) minute show which will consist of approximately 3 to 5 songs. You also want to invite DJ's who you will be relying on to play your music at the clubs and street teams (who may have or will in the future help you promote your music). Invite concert promoters who may use your group as opening acts on large concert tours.

People of importance in the industry and some outside the industry are who you depend on or may depend on in the future.

This will be a small showcase of the talent that is on the album. Throughout the night you would like to have the first single played at least 3 to 4 times. The CD release party is just a pre-show for your CD, which should be released the next day or at least 1 to 3 days after the party. You can also use this release party to sell your CD's so your best route would be to have them already in the stores.

"An error doesn't have to become a mistake until you refuse to correct it."

CHAPTER 10

SOME OF THE MOST FREQUENTLY ASKED QUESTIONS.

"Money never starts an idea, it is the idea that starts the money."

Darrell Ballard

Where do I find an in-house producer?

First, in order to have an in-house producer you have to create one. Most independent labels want their own producer so you would have to buy and provide all the equipment your producer will need. It's like hiring for any position except in this case instead of putting ads in the paper, put the word on the streets that you are interested in producers.

Who do I contact to produce CD's, vinyls, posters, etc.?

You can write to me directly and I will find either the companies close to your area or a company that will meet your requirements and needs.

How do I negotiate a contract?

Contracts vary, so write to me to discuss the specific contract. All contracts are not the same.

How to gain money to promote a concert?

One way is to get sponsors to back you or you can try to print tickets for presale and sell the amount of tickets needed to cover the cost.

How much to spend on production?

That is a good one. You want to spend as little as possible but at the same time you want to get good music. Set a budget on your total project on what you can afford. Then break it down since you already have some idea of some of the cost.

How much to pay an artist?

Remember that you must re-coop all of the money that you put into a project first before you begin to pay anybody out of your profits. The price on paying varies on the degree of how hard the artist works. That would be something

I wouldn't want to put a price on until we discuss it in more detail.

Who do I contact about getting my songs on vinyl?

If you want a company close to you I would have to know your specific location.

How many vinyl copies should I start with?

My suggestion would be 100 pieces.

What should be my next step after receiving my vinyls?

Locate your local record pool of DJ's and supply each one with two copies of your vinyls.

What kind of deal should I be looking for?

A distribution deal or label deal.

Who would I contact about a promotion deal?

The concert promoters

What types of promotions should I pursue?

The first form of promotion should be street promotions.

Should a person buy and build an in-house studio to record their music?

No, at first when beginning your label you want to save money and make money, so spend as little as possible.

Because I consult many groups, labels and companies, it may be best for you to contact me and my firm first to see if

I associate or do business with the party you are interested in doing business with for a possible discount.

Darrell Ballard

"Failure is not the worst thing in the world the very worst is not to try."

"The greatest thing in this world is not so much where we are, but in what direction we are moving in."

Darrell Ballard

I hope I have answered most of your questions, but if you have a question that I did not go over, feel free to write me directly and I will contact you and get you the answers you need. If you would like to contact or work with anybody in particular, write to me regarding contact names or companies you are interested in and I will negotiate for you. Feel free to write and talk to me about your music business. I'm here for consulting. I will represent you.

Please feel free to write me at the address below.

CONSULTING EXPRESS
(Music Consultants)
P.O. BOX 413
ST. LOUIS, MO. 63033

You can also call 314-741-2825

HOLLA DINK!

"Wisdom comes with age but sometimes age comes alone."

From the book " Words of Wisdom"
By
Darrell (Dink) Ballard

OTHER BOOKS BY THE AUTHOR INCLUDE

Words of Wisdom
Secrets to Success
The Benefits of Incorporating

TO PURCHASE FOR OTHERS TO SHARE

TO ORDER INDIVIDUAL COPIES OF THE BOOK: TELEPHONE CONSULTING EXPRESS AT 314-741-2825 OR SEND $10.00 CHECK OR MONEY ORDER TO:

CONSULTING EXPRESS
P.O. BOX 413
ST. LOUIS, MO. 63033

HOW TO START
A
RECORD LABEL

BY: DINK
A.K.A.
DARRELL BALLARD

Printed in the United Kingdom
by Lightning Source UK Ltd.
106485UKS00001B/24